There Is No Such Thing as Cultural Identity

François Jullien

Translated by Pedro Rodriguez

T0087491

polity

Originally published in French as *Il n'y a pas d'identité culturelle* © Editions de l'Herne, 2016.
Published by arrangement with Agence littéraire Astier-Pécher. ALL RIGHTS RESERVED.

This English edition © 2021 by Polity Press

Polity Press
65 Bridge Street
Cambridge CB2 1UR, UK

Polity Press
101 Station Landing
Suite 300
Medford, MA 02155, USA

ISBN-13: 978-1-5095-4698-5- hardback
ISBN-13: 978-1-5095-4699-2- paperback

A catalogue record for this book is available from the British Library.

Library of Congress Cataloging-in-Publication Data

Names: Jullien, François, 1951- author. | Rodríguez, Pedro, 1974 March
    24- translator.
Title: There is no such thing as cultural identity / François Jullien ;
    translated by Pedro Rodriguez.
Other titles: Il n'y a pas d'identité culturelle. English.
Description: Cambridge ; Medford, MA : Polity Press, [2021] | "Originally
    published in French as Il n'y a pas d'identité culturelle (c) Editions
    de l'Herne, 2016." | Includes bibliographical references. | Summary: "A
    powerful critique of our preoccupation with identity and difference"--
    Provided by publisher.
Identifiers: LCCN 2020041249 (print) | LCCN 2020041250 (ebook) | ISBN
    9781509546985 (hardback) | ISBN 9781509546992 (paperback) | ISBN
    9781509547005 (epub) | ISBN 9781509547036 (pdf)
Subjects: LCSH: National characteristics, French. | Group identity--France.
    | Nationalism--France. | Social values--France.
Classification: LCC DC34 .J8513 2021 (print) | LCC DC34 (ebook) | DDC
    306.0944--dc23
LC record available at https://lccn.loc.gov/2020041249
LC ebook record available at https://lccn.loc.gov/2020041250

Typeset in 12.5 on 15 pt Adobe Garamond by
Servis Filmsetting Ltd, Stockport, Cheshire
Printed and bound in the UK by Short Run Press Ltd

The publisher has used its best endeavours to ensure that the URLs for external websites referred to in this book are correct and active at the time of going to press. However, the publisher has no responsibility for the websites and can make no guarantee that a site will remain live or that the content is or will remain appropriate.

Every effort has been made to trace all copyright holders, but if any have been overlooked the publisher will be pleased to include any necessary credits in any subsequent reprint or edition.

For further information on Polity, visit our website: politybooks.com

There Is No Such Thing as Cultural Identity

Contents

Preface   vi

I   The universal, the uniform, the common   1
II   Is the universal an outmoded notion?   8
III   Difference or divide: identity or
      fecundity   23
IV   There is no such thing as cultural
      identity   32
V   We will defend a culture's resources   39
VI   From divides to the common   53
VII   Dia-logue   63

Translator's Notes   76

Preface

France's next election campaign,[1] they tell us, will come down to "cultural identity."

It will turn on such questions as: Shouldn't we defend France's "cultural identity" against the self-segregation of various communities?[2] and Where do we draw the line between tolerance and assimilation, acceptance of differences and identitarian demands?

This is a debate that is occurring throughout Europe and, more generally, concerns the relationship between cultures within the schema of globalization.

But I think it starts with a conceptual error. It cannot be a matter of culture-isolating "differences" but of divides [*écarts*] that keep cultures apart but also face to face, in tension, and thereby promote a common [*du commun*] between them. This is a matter not of identity, as cultures by their nature shift and transform, but of fecundities, or what I will call resources.

Rather than defend any French cultural identity, as anything of the sort would be impossible to identify, I will defend French (European) cultural resources – "defend" meaning not so much protect as exploit. Resources arise in a language just as they do within a tradition, in a certain milieu and landscape. Once we understand this such resources become available to all and no longer belong [*n'appartiennent pas*]. Resources are not exclusive, in the manner of "values"; they are not to be "extolled" or "preached." We deploy them or do not, activate them or let them fall into escheat. For this each of us bears responsibility.

A conceptual shift of this kind requires us to head upstream and redefine three rival terms – the universal, the uniform, the common – to draw them out of their equivocalness. In like manner, it will behoove us to head downstream and rethink the "dia-logue" of cultures: *dia* from divide [*écart*] and progress [*cheminement*],[3] *logos* from the common of the intelligible. For it is the common of the intelligible that yields the human.

Should we confuse our concepts we will bog down in a false debate, head straight away for an impasse.

I

The universal, the uniform, the common

We should specify our terms on entering this debate, lest we flounder about. There are three rivals: the universal, the uniform, and the common. These are easily conflated, but we must also strip each of its attendant equivocality. Sitting atop our triangle is *the universal*, for which we must distinguish two meanings, or else fail to understand both the reasons for its *trenchancy* and its societal import. One meaning of the universal we will call weak, a matter of observation, limited to experience. Such-and-such, as we have been able observe until now, has always been as it seems. This is the general sense. It poses no problem and is in no way striking. But the universal has a strong meaning as well: that of strict or rigorous universality. We in Europe have made this sort of universality into a requirement of thought. We presume from the start, before seeking any confirmation from experience, or even dispensing with confirmation altogether, that such-and-such *must* be so. Not only has it always seemed so, but it cannot be otherwise. This sort of "universal" is not general; it is necessary. It is universal not in fact but ineluctably (*a priori*). It is not comparative but absolute, not so much extensive as imperative. It was on this strong, rigorous universality that the Greeks founded the possibility of science, and that seventeenth-century Europe, effecting a transference from mathematics to physics (Newton), conceived "universal laws of nature" – to spectacular and well-known effect.

Hence the question that has divided modernity: is the rigorous sort of universality – to which science owes its power, which imposes logical necessity on natural phenomena, and mathematics on physics – applicable to behavior as well? Is it equally pertinent in the domain of ethics? Is our behavior subject to the absolute necessity of moral, "categorical" (Kantian) imperatives, like the *a priori* necessity that has rewarded physics with its inarguable success? Or must we follow Nietzsche and Kierkegaard in the separate domain of morality, in the (secret) recess of our inner experience, and claim for ourselves the opposite of the universal: the *individual* or the *singular*? In the sphere of subjects, and of society more generally, the universal as a term remains equivocal. The question is therefore all the more pressing. When we speak of "universal history"[1] (or of a "universal exposition"[2]) we mean universal in the sense of a totality or generality, not of necessity. But does the same apply when we speak of the universal rights of man? Is the necessity we accord to the rights of man not ascribed in principle? What legitimacy does this necessity have? Is it not improperly imposed?

A pressing question, as we have since undergone a significant experience – indeed, one of the decisive experiences of our time. As we have now discovered in our encounters with other cultures, the requirement of universality that has carried science along, and that classical morality has demanded, is anything but universal. It is in fact quite singular – that is, the opposite of universal – because, at least when taken to the European extreme of necessity, peculiar to

3

the cultural history of Europe. To begin with, how should we translate "universal" outside of Europe? With this question the requirement of universality, which we had comfortably stowed within the *credo* of our certainties, among the most obvious of our precepts, once again becomes salient. It emerges before our eyes from its banality. It reappears as an inventive, audacious, even adventurous thing. And, we find, it takes on outside Europe a fascinating strangeness.

The notion of the *uniform* is itself equivocal. One might believe it the accomplishment and realization of the universal. But it is in fact the universal's reverse – or, I would say, its perversion. For the uniform derives not from reason, like the universal, but from production: it is merely standard and stereotype. It proceeds not from necessity but from convenience. The uniform is, after all, cheaper to produce. Whereas the universal is "turned toward the One," toward its ideal end, the uniform is but a repetition of the one, identically "formed" and no longer inventive. Today the perils of confusing the uniform with the universal are increasing, because with globalization we see the same things reproduced and distributed throughout the world. Because we see only them, because they have come to saturate the landscape, we are tempted to ascribe to these uniform things the legitimacy of the universal – a necessity of principle – when in fact they result from a mere extension of the market, and their reason for being is purely economic. Ways of life, objects and goods, discourse and opinion are becoming uniform all around the planet, through the explosion in technology and media, but this does not make them universal. Even if ubiquitous they would lack a need to be [*devoir être*].

Whereas the universal relates to logic, and the uniform to economics, the *common* is of political dimension. The common is what is shared. On its foundations the Greeks erected their concept of the Polis. Unlike the uniform, the common is not the similar. This is a crucial distinction today. Under globalization's imposed regime of uniformity we are tempted to reduce the common to the similar: that is, to engage in *assimilation*. We must instead promote the common *that is not the similar*. Only this manner of common is productive. This is the common that I will be calling for, because only a common that is not the similar is effective. Or, as Braque said, "the common is true, the similar false. Trouillebert," as he went on to illustrate, "resembles Corot, but they have nothing in common." This is indeed the crux of the matter today, whatever the scale at which we consider the common: whether Polis, nation, or humanity. The common of a community can be active only if we promote a common that does not reduce to the uniform. Only then can it effectively provide something to share.

On the other side of our theoretical triangle, and unlike the universal, the common will not be established by fiat. But it is, in part, given. Such is the common of my family or of my "nation," which devolves to me by birth. In addition, the common is decided and is the proper object of a choice. This is the common of a political movement, an association, a party, or any collective engagement. This shared common is, as such, distributed bit by bit. I hold something in common with my loved ones, with my countrymen, and with those who speak my language, but also with all men, even with the entire animal kingdom, and, still more broadly, with all life – this last and vastest common being the purview of ecology. All sharing of the common is in effect, and in principle, extensive. But this "common" remains as such equivocal, because the limit that defines the interior of the sharing can flip into its opposite. It can flip into a border that excludes all others from the common. By the same token, then, the *inclusive* reveals itself to be, in reverse, *exclusive*. Shutting itself in, it expels to the outside. This is the common that verges on intolerance, the self-segregation of communities known as *communautarisme*.[3]

II

Is the universal an outmoded notion?

The concept of the universal, which in its strong sense carried European culture through its development, is today entangled in difficulties – and in two respects. Our encounters with other cultures have, for one thing, shown it to be self-contradictory, the product of a singular history of thought. What's more, however, the singular history from which the universal proceeds in Europe itself lacks the character of necessity implied in its very principle. As soon as we shift away from a properly philosophical perspective and consider its notional origins within the (more general) cultural development of what Europe would become we realize the extent to which the advent of the universal stems from a composite, not to say chaotic, history. It stems from various levels, at times opposed, and whose inner links we struggle to perceive. I will cite at least three: the philosophical (Greek) level of the concept, the juridical (Roman) level of citizenship, and the religious (Christian) level of salvation. What "necessary" relation links them? And does it amount to a "history"? We must at least sketch out an *archaeology*[1] to sound the strata from which European universality formed and decide whether we still hold to it. If we do not begin to elucidate this history, our political debate will remain forever haunted. Indeed, will debate even be possible?

The point of departure is clear: the first level of the universal's advent as a concept is the level of concepts itself. In other words, the promotion of the notion of the universal into a concept gets muddled with the promotion of the concept into a philosophical tool. In Europe we are born to this heritage. The Greeks sought in the beginning to speak of the "whole" [*le « tout »*] of the world. They sought in a peremptory, so very hasty gesture to grasp this "whole" with the mind. Were they going to call it "water," "air," or the "unlimited"? Unable to agree on the whole, or even on its principle, they converted their thinking; rather

9

than consider the totality that escaped them, they considered the *mode of the whole*, "on the whole" [« *selon le tout* »] (*kath'holou*, from which "catholic" derives): in the manner of concepts, or, in other words, of the universal. The history of philosophy traces this change to Socrates. Rather than seek to determine which things are beautiful, or what is beautiful, we would seek to understand *beauty* [*le beau*]. What is beauty in itself as a unitary whole, abstracted from the diverse? What is beauty's essence? What is the beauty we see dispersed in the many beautiful and varied things we have before our eyes? In other words, Beauty as a universal or concept. On the opening page of his *Metaphysics* Aristotle leads us to set aside the individuality of sensation that we might rise to the abstract universal that is the stuff of knowledge. This universal becomes, in Europe, the foundation of science. It will be science's requirement. Whereas common opinion views things in the manner of contingency – that is, of what could be other than it is – science views things in the manner of necessity, and therefore of the universal – that is, of what cannot be otherwise.

What were the consequences of this for us (Europeans)? What destiny has it laid down? If science, in its demands, differs from the common regime of opinion it is not because its affirmations are true or false, for there are true opinions as well. It is because of the necessary character that attends to scientific affirmations once they accede to universality. But what does science irredeemably set aside in its elevation to the universal? Here there would seem to be a limb that only Greek, in all of human history, has ventured out onto. What have we *left behind* by attaching ourselves to the universal? Is it only an apparent diversity (let's call it instead the diversity of appearance)? Or is it instead the individual (or the singular), the *stuff of experience*? As Aristotle already remarks, it is indeed a particular man that we care for, this or that man, "each" as he is, and not man in general. Hence the self-perplexity that redounds to philosophy, the perplexity with its own enterprise of abstraction "towards" the universal, or of conceptualization. Philosophy would seem to have abandoned effective reality, the sort that exists only in the singular. But have we emerged, if only slightly, from these misgivings today? According to an adage of Aristotle's, science is about universals, *de universalibus* – "about" implying remove, as if we were only in the neighborhood[2] – whereas "existence" is made of individuals: *existentia est singularum*; we apprehend it only in the unicity of the singular. The result has been a divorce and perhaps trauma for European culture, heir to the injunction to think in universals. But there was a compensation: the European vocation of literature. Science and philosophy having taken up the quest of following the injunction, literature recovered what the universal had set aside: the *individual*. Literature evokes *an* emotion, recounts "a life." At the same time, it recovers the *ambiguous*, which is inherent to life itself and was set aside by the *absolute*, the child of abstraction.

The universal promoted by Rome developed on another level and thus has a different nature, a different heritage. It is linked to the necessity implied by the *law* as imposed on a vast empire. Despite its immense conquests, Rome was never set up as a nation or State. It was always conceived of within the traditional framework of the Polis, and could therefore only extend its particular framework of citizenship, gradually, to the limits of its world. In other words, Rome's historical importance lies in the extended sharing of its citizenship until (with the Edict of Carcalla, in

212) it became common to the whole empire, and the city and the world, *urbs et orbis*, were bound by a single legal tie. The world city of the Stoics remained an essentially moral concept, upheld by the sole figure of the Wise Man and fusion with the cosmos. It had no political import. In Rome, however, "universal citizenship," *civitas universa*, starts to become effective. Through the law the universal emerges from philosophy, sheds the sheath of logic, and defines a unit of status and condition. One is a citizen of one's city and of Rome as well. One has a "small" as well as a "large" country. The former is "natural," local, geographic. The latter has to do with citizenship, for what is "Roman" is not a given; the Roman is what constructs the juridical tie. "Rome" is no longer content to be an individual city. By this universal dimension it erects itself into the "world's second mother," *parens mundi altera.*

Within the limits of its *limes* Rome is a first, rather successful example of "globalization." But what does Christianity contribute to this – or fracture in it? Against this reign of legality, be it civic or religious, Roman or Jewish, what will in time become Christianity founds a new universal: not of law but of faith. Not by addition [*en*

plein], as in the framework of Roman citizenship, but by subtraction [*en creux*]: by an inner
hollowing out [*évidement intérieur*] of all that
is not the universal of God's grace and love.
Only these can fill what is thereby promoted
as the interiority of the subject; only they can
fulfill it and even cause it to "spill over [*déborder*]." Christianity is notably peculiar for having
spread in a language other than the one Christ
preached in (Aramaic). The Gospels are written in Greek, which Christ did not speak and,
what's more, is not just any other language. It is
the language of the philosophical universal. This
makes the parallel between (Greek) "wisdom"
and the "madness" of the Cross (*sophía/mōría*),
and the former's reversal by the latter, all the
more significant. But Paul was an important
promoter of universals also because he purged
Christianity's message of anecdote from Christ's
life and severed its dependence on the Jewish
milieu. He thereby withdrew and neutralized all
divisions, whether of race (culture), sex, or condition. "There is neither Jew nor Greek, there is
neither bond nor free, there is neither male nor
female."[3] Instead, all are included in the same
status of children of God and are one in Jesus

14

Christ. Faith in Christ, then, radically changes man's condition. At the same time, it pulls men from their differences and sets them up in an equality of principle, for all are called to the same inner conversion in following their respective paths as singular subjects. From this point we can begin to envisage a *universal of subjects*.

Hence the founding of a universal in the strong sense of the term, to rival philosophy's: the universal not of *concepts* but of *belief*. Belief now takes precedence over all else, triumphs over all else, and God is suddenly no longer the God of any people in particular. Not only is this universal held aloft by divinity and its providential design, it is also the universal of the announced Event. Christ's resurrection (victory over death) is the pure, absolute event, delivered from all anecdote, and absorbing into itself all other events. The Christian message, by God's plan and the Economy of Salvation, is meant to be valid for all men and for eternity. It remained only to articulate the universal's transcendence – which is also the eternity of Truth – with the individual in History and his temporal existence. This is already accomplished in Christ's incarnation. Conceived as both totally man and totally God,

Christ unites (reconciles) in himself the two opposites: the universal and the singular. This incarnation of the universal in the singular is transposed to the Church; then secularized in the Great Man (Hegel: Napoleon is the "world spirit on horseback," then Prussia . . .); then deposited in a class, the proletariat, which will emancipate humanity (Marx); and then ascribed to a culture: "Western" civilization, the self-declared stand-ard-bearer of "universal values."

The West's pretensions to the universal are, of course, no longer tenable. I say "the West" and not "Europe" because the West exceeds Europe geographically, but also because as a notion the West is ideological, and not, like Europe, his-torical: "the West" as a power, a seat of values, and a hegemon. With loss of hegemony, how-ever, the universalism that the West pretends to embody, and that power alone had imposed, has fallen into discredit. Our encounters with other cultures have forced us to ask whether the Western aspiration to the universal is itself universal. Moreover, because it stems from vari-ous levels (at least three: conceptual abstraction, citizenship, salvation), we must ask whether we don't require universality as a compensation:

whether in demanding it we don't seek to neu-
tralize the multi-level fracture. Whether it wasn't
meant to "hold together" so many heterogeneous, even contradictory things – science / the law
/ faith – that we had to hoist the universal into
the keystone slot, and make its logical legitimacy
into a demand in every way universal. Would
a more integrated, more homogeneous culture
than Europe's need this *tenon* of universality?
We must retrospectively ask the question, must
introspect, if we seriously hope to conceive of a
future for Europe, and especially for what constitutes "Europe." But does it therefore follow that
the requirement of the universal as promoted in
Europe has reached its expiry? Does it follow that
the requirement, having partaken in History as a
"Western" value, and imposed itself by force on
other cultures, can no longer serve to promote
or be invoked? Or should we comb through the
historical legacy of the universal and redefine its
potential validity?

One thing, at least, is certain: one form of
universality – that of totalization or comple-
tion – is indeed no longer valid. In believing we
have attained the universal we are in fact failing to
realize what said universality lacks. In the Ghent

Altarpiece the Van Eyck brothers painted all the crowds of the world converging on the altar of the Mystic Lamb. Enthroned above is a God who resembles both the Father and the Son, and in the background are city walls that might just as easily be Jerusalem's or Ghent's. This altarpiece is a fine example of an expired universal, not only for its Apocalyptic message but also because its panorama has no clue what its pretended totality lacks. It deems itself accomplished, definitively advened, and gives no thought to what might be missing. It rests on its positivity and opens the way to no further progress. No longer serving to promote, it is satisfied. For a century we spoke in like manner of "universal" suffrage with nary a thought to the exclusion of women.

In other words, the *universal* is to be conceived in opposition to *universalism*, which imposes its sovereignty and believes itself to possess universality. The universality we must fight for is, on the contrary, rebellious, and never fulfilled. Let's call it a negative universality that spoils the comfort of all stilled positivity. Rather than totalize (saturate), it reopens the lack in any achieved totality. A *regulatory* universality (in the Kantian sense) that, because never satisfied, is always pushing back the horizon and extending the quest. This universal is precious on both a theoretical and a political plane. It is, notably, this universal that we must demand in order to deploy *the common*; for it is this concern for the universal that takes whatever ideality it contains and promotes it into a never-to-be-attained ideal, thereby calling on the common not to limit its scope so soon. It is this universal that we must invoke if the *sharing* of the common is to remain open and not flip into a border, not reverse into its own opposite: the exclusion that leads to the self-segregation of communities [*communautarisme*].

There nevertheless arises a preliminary question, a doubt cast on the universal right where we thought it unassailable: in its very logic. Are any notions *universal from the outset*? Traditional philosophy has not hesitated to say yes, but our encounters with other cultures lead us today to ask the question anew. Are there, in other words, root concepts to all human understanding, concepts to which the full diversity of cultures and thought might, in principle, be subject? We tend to believe it (I myself have believed it) as long as we remain inside European language. (Kant's table of "categories," like a table of laws for the mind as well as for language, serves as the "dem-onstration.") But I have now spent considerable time in a culture outside of European language and tradition – namely, China's – and am no longer so sure. The concept of "substance," for example, is held to be universal, but is it neces-sary, or even possible, in a language like Chinese, which offers no "being" ("To be or not to be") but only predication? A language that is never concerned with the inherent "being" of things? (The Chinese word for "thing" is "east-west," *dong-xi*, and thus refers less to an essence than to a relation.) Some will object that this is just a manner of speaking, but a manner of speak-ing is *also* (and primarily) a manner of thinking. Or consider the distinction between unity and plurality. Is this original to, and thus universal in, a language like Chinese, which lacks morphol-ogy and thus needn't necessarily (grammatically) choose between the plural and the singular? And what of the distinction between "existence" and "non-existence"? Is it universal and endowed with logical necessity if one learns to think, as Chinese thought encourages us to do, of the eminently "subtle" stage of *transition* (something of which Europe has scarcely any notion)? If we learn to paint between "there is" and "there is not," to paint the twilight or the fog, in the manner of a Chinese scholar?

The universal, then, is not something we encounter right away, or at least we are not guaranteed to encounter it. It is not *given*. It is not a soft pillow on which to lay our heads. Nothing suggests that we can array the diversity of languages and cultures beneath the "universal" categories that European knowledge has set up over the course of its history. But the universal can spur us to inquiry if we project it before us like a horizon, a horizon never to be reached, an ideal never to be met. Set forth as a requirement it will encourage cultures not to withdraw into their "differences," not to be content with their supposed "essence," but to keep themselves turned out – *outstretched* [*tendues*][4] – towards other cultures, other languages, other lines of thought. And thus to continue reworking themselves [*se retravailler*][5] to meet the requirement, and therefore also to change – that is, to stay alive (as we have already said of languages that are not "dead"). A universal that is never satisfied is what keeps cultures face to face [*en regard*] across so many divides, thanks to which they can reflect and influence one another. Rather than be shut within their "identity" they can discover their respective fecundities, and be called to reconfigure themselves in consequence. This goes not just for the languages and cultures spread over the planet's surface but also for the cultural diversity that exists within single countries – as is increasingly the case, notably in Europe. The two are inseparable. We cannot consider the one without considering the other. Culture's inherent diversity, inner as well as outer, gives rise to a single fundamental question, a *political* question: how can we take this diversity, which lies at the origin of culture and constitutes its resource, and produce with it the *common* necessary both to *deploy* the human, in extension of its possibilities, and to "live together"?

III

Difference or divide: identity or fecundity

We can now restate the question. The *universality that keeps the common open* might easily fold back into the self-segregation of communities. How, then, shall we think through its opposite: the *singularity* of cultures, the singularity of both languages and lines of thought? How shall we connect the two? How shall we approach cultural diversity once we have prevented its erasure through the standardization of the *uniform* and saved *the common* from confusion with *the similar*? Ordinarily we deal in terms of "difference" and "identity," an old pair that comes down to us from philosophy and has clearly been operative in the realm of knowledge since the Greeks. But is it suitable for our present debate? Need we account for the diversity of cultures in differential terms and by specific traits, holding these to be characteristic, and then infer the identity of each culture we thereby distinguish? There is, I fear, a conceptual error in this, as I have already said. And with inadequate concepts our debate can go nowhere. Suffice it to say, any debate on cultural "identity" is, I think, doomed from the start. I therefore propose a conceptual shift. I suggest we approach the diversity of cultures by substituting an exploratory *divide* [*écart*] for difference, and *resource* or *fecundity* for identity. This is no semantic refinement. We are introducing a divergence – let us already call it a divide – to reconfigure the debate: to pull it from its rut and reengage with it more securely.

How to differentiate the exploratory divide from difference if in fact we begin by identifying each (begin from the standpoint, that is, of knowledge)? Both mark a separation, but difference does it through *distinction*, the divide through *distance*. *Difference*, then, is classificatory – its analysis proceeding by resemblance and difference – and at the same time identificatory. It is by proceeding "from difference to difference," as Aristotle says, that we

24

arrive at a final difference. This final difference delivers the essence of the thing, expressed in a definition. The *divide*, by contrast, is not identificatory but exploratory, giving rise to some other possibility. Thus a divide has no classifying function – does not set up typologies, in the manner of a difference – but consists precisely in the overflowing of classes. Rather than an orderly array, it produces *disarray* [*non pas un rangement, mais un* dérangement]. We commonly speak of "taking a detour [*faire un écart*]" (and wonder: "How far off is the detour going to take us [*jusqu'où va l'écart*]?").[1] We leave behind the norm and the ordinary. Such are the divides of language or behavior. The divide stands in opposition also to the expected, the foreseeable, the settled. Whereas difference aims to describe and, to this end, proceeds by *determination* (the distinction and "analysis" of essences, as the Greeks recommended), the divide *prospects*: it imagines – fathoms – how far we might clear other paths. It is adventurous.

Let us further detail the difference in question: "difference" because here, at the start, I am indeed taking the analytic perspective of knowledge, precisely to establish an operative divide.

A divide, in other words, that will separate me from the unthought-of [*l'impensé*] in the debate over cultural difference, from the cause of its bogging down, so that we can get a new handle on things. Insofar as it proceeds by distinction, difference separates one specimen from others and establishes its specificity by comparison. It both supposes a nearby genre with which to mark a difference and ends up determining an identity. Is this a suitable approach to the diversity of cultures? Difference will cast aside the second term once it has distinguished one term from another. Suppose, like Plato in his pedagogical (ironic) mode, that I sought to define an angler. I would begin by distinguishing between the activities of production and acquisition, retaining acquisition and casting aside production. Then, within acquisition, I would distinguish between exchange and capture, retaining capture and casting aside exchange. Then I would consider the objects of capture and distinguish between the animate and the inanimate, retaining the animate and casting aside the inanimate. And so on. Proceeding from difference to difference I would reach a definition (of an "angler"). With each comparison I would retain only one of the terms and throw out the other. With difference, once a distinction is made, each of the two terms forgets the other; each goes its own way.

With a *divide*, however, the two separated terms remain face to face. This is why divides are precious to thought. The distance that appears between separated terms maintains tension between them. But what do we mean by "tension"? With difference each of the two terms turns placidly back to its business once the relation effected by comparison has concluded; each shuts itself back into its specificity. With a divide, meanwhile, the confrontation of the two terms endures through the distance that appears between them; each remains open to the other, is kept in tension by the other, and must be apprehending itself continually in the face-off. The vis-à-vis is never undone. The *face-off* endures, forever keen; it remains intensive. In other words, with difference each of the two compared terms can simply fold back in on itself once it has allowed its essence to be discerned by opposition, once it has been apprehended in its purity. Whereas with a divide the separated terms are kept in tension by each other. "By" here is active. Each must continually measure itself against the other; each "hangs" on the other. They are continually discovering themselves in the divide, both exploring and reflecting themselves through it. Each remains dependent on the other for its self-knowledge and cannot fold back on its supposed identity. Consequently, through the distance opened between the one and the other, the divide brings forth an "interspace" [*de l'« entre »*], and this *interspace* is active. With difference, where each term goes back to its own business, separating from the other the better to identify its own identity, no "interspace" opens and nothing further happens. However, with the divide, and the *interspace* opened by the appearing distance, each term – rather than fold back into itself, rather than rest on its self – remains turned toward the other, set in tension by the other. In this respect, then, the divide is ethical and political in vocation. In the *interspace* opened between the two an intensity deploys such that the one causes the other to spill over [*déborder*]. The intensity puts them to work [*les fait travailler*]: one can already sense benefits accruing to the relation between cultures.

It is true that we do not know how to think out "interspace." *Interspace* is not "being," and for this reason its thought has long escaped us. The Greeks, because they thought about Being, because they thought in terms of "Being," in terms of determination and properties, were horrified by the in-determinate. They proved unable to think about "interspace," which is neither the one nor the other but, instead, a place where each is spilled over by its other, dispossessed of its own in-itself and "properties." (Unable to think of the "interspace," *metaxu*, they thought instead of the "beyond" – *meta* – of "meta-physics.") *Interspace*, being neither the one nor the other, has no in-itself, no essence, no nature. Properly speaking, the *interspace* "is" not. But it is nonetheless not "neutral": that is, not inoperative. It is in the "interspace," the in-between that is opened by the divide and thereafter resists resorption, that "something" effectively passes (happens)[2] to breach the enclosures of belonging and properties – the properties we build up through difference – and thus undo identity. To begin thinking about interspace, then, we must step outside the thought of Being (outside ontology), tread where painters trod before philosophers. Braque once more: "What lies between the apple and the dish is to be painted as well."

Difference, meanwhile, is bound inexorably to identity – and in two ways, at both ends. First, at its point of origin, upstream, it presumes a common genre, a shared identity, and marks a specification within it. Second, at its point of arrival, in its aim and destination, it compels the determination of an identity, settling on an essence and its definition. In this, as I have said, difference is identificatory. Even in linguistics, where it is set forth as primary and separate from resemblance, difference never veers from the differential function of identification. From it stem properties established as characteristics, and thus the very possibility of knowledge. The divide, however, shifts us away from the identificatory perspective. It brings forth not an identity but what I will call a "fecundity," or, to put it another way, a *resource*. In opening up, the divide gives rise to another possibility. It leads us to discover other resources, ones not yet considered or even suspected. By leaving aside the expected, the agreed-to (by "taking a detour [*faire un écart*]"), by detaching from the well-known, the divide [*l'écart*], unsettling as it is, brings to light "something" that has hitherto escaped our thinking. In this it is fecund. It does not give rise to knowledge, through classification. Rather, it prompts reflection through the tension it sets up. In the *interspace* that it opens – the active, inventive *interspace* – the divide prompts work, because the two terms that stand apart in it, and that it holds face to face, will ceaselessly inquire into themselves in the resulting gulf. Each remains concerned with the other and does not close itself off. Perhaps this, and not a withdrawal into "differences," would better serve a relation between cultures.

IV

There is no such thing as cultural identity

From the conceptual distinction between a divide and difference we should begin to perceive why there can be no such thing as cultural identity – and, in the first place, why viewing the diversity of cultures from the perspective of difference leads inexorably to an impasse. An impasse both up- and downstream from difference, if we find identity at either end. Upstream from whatever cultural differences we set forth, logic will compel us to presume a preliminary identity – a common, unitary, primordial genre – from which the diversity of cultures could unfold. What is this common ("nearby") genre from which our various cultures should spring as so many specific differences? Shall we call it "Man" or "human nature"? We will be hard pressed to ascribe credible – that is, non-ideological – content to either of these representations. But what else could we project to lie upstream from cultural differences, such that they might unfold from it like a fan? We might say "common ground," as others have done, but this is just another naive name for the great X that, once we adopt the logic of difference, we cannot do without. Taking this step is conditional, as it were, on a sacrifice before the myth of monism and the Original One.

For it is readily apparent that culture, at whatever scale we consider it, is by nature plural and singular *at the same time*. To say it in reverse, we must rid ourselves of the convenient representation – itself indelibly mythological – according to which there was at the start a cultural unity-identity that only *later* diversified, by malediction (Babel) or, at least, complication (through proliferation). Hence the diversity of our languages, which is in no way a posterior phenomenon. I would say instead that culture by its nature deploys in the tension – or divide – between the plural and the unitary; that it is caught in a double, contrary movement of hetero- and homogenization; that it is compelled both to fuse with and to break away from, to dis-identify and to re-identify itself, to conform and to resist. In short, there can be no dominant culture unless a dissident (underground, "off,"[1] etc.) culture forms in tandem. For where does "culture" come from if not precisely from the tension of the diverse that the divide produces: that the divide spurs into work and thus also into continual mutation?

Downstream too, to examine the diverse in terms of difference is to seek to isolate and fix each culture in its identity. But this is impossible, because culture by its nature mutates and transforms. This is a monumental reason, pertaining to culture's very essence. A culture that no longer transforms is a dead culture. (We speak the same way of dead languages: those that have ceased evolving, because no longer spoken.) *Transformation* lies at the root of culture, which is why we cannot establish cultural characteristics or speak of a culture's identity. How are we to characterize French culture? How are we to fix its identity? Shall we chalk it up to La Fontaine or to Rimbaud? To René Descartes or to André Breton? French culture is no more the one than the other, but it is, of course, in the *divide* between them: *in* the tension between the two, or, let us say, in the *interspace* that opens between them. It is the *interspace* open between them – vast and vertiginous – that constitutes the riches, or what we will call the *resource*, of French culture.

The two figures elucidate each other, simultaneously, through their divide, each coming to a greater understanding of itself through the other, in their face-off. Passing from one to the other, we better understand La Fontaine through Rimbaud, and Descartes through Breton. The divide opened by Rimbaud causes La Fontaine to splash back, draws him out of the banality that our routine (grade-school) reading of him, verging on cliché, has established. Rimbaud helps us discover La Fontaine in his own inventiveness. Rediscovered through the divide with Rimbaud, La Fontaine regains his former singularity, even his strangeness. In like manner, the divide opened by surrealism puts tension back into our rationalism, compelling us to see anew just how daring and adventurous rationalism was: and how many perils it held for the mind – not how ordinary but how inventive it really is. If instead we favor the one, we reduce the other to a mere exception – exceptions being, of course, things we cannot account for. Or else we come to see that the apparent exception, by opening a divide with the norm (with the expected and the established), turns out to be the most interesting thing within a culture, because the most significant or creative.

We must reckon the cost of our conceptual errors. We must gauge the danger – the political danger – of examining the diversity of cultures in terms of differences and identity: the cost not only for thought but also for History. Samuel P. Huntington's *The Clash of Civilizations* is in this respect instructive. The book describes what are presumed to be the world's chief cultures (the "Chinese," the "Islamic," the "Western") in terms of differences and thus of identity, lays down their traits, and then tabulates and organizes those traits into a typology. This convenient method no doubt accounts for much of the book's success, as it disturbs nothing, opens no divide with what has been agreed to. It undoes none of the clichés – the prejudices – to which we are content to reduce cultures so as not to have to bother with them anymore. When we fail to recognize the heterogeneity of every culture (its internal "heterotopia," in other words) – fail to recognize the very thing that deploys it, via divide, from the interior and intensifies it – we are both taking the easy road of classification and reassuring ourselves. But do cultures have a "hard core," a pure center? Huntington grasps nothing of interest about these cultures. He reduces them to banalities, isolates them from one another, walls them up in their supposed specificities and most salient differences, folds them back into their identities. He therefore cannot help but end up at the "clash" of his title.

That there has been a cost, some damage, we can see by looking, closer to home, at the failure of Europe. In drafting a preamble to the European Constitution we sought to define Europe, to come to some agreement on its identity. But European identity turned out to be impossible to define. It led to an impasse. Is Europe Christian, as some have defined it (invoking "its Christian roots": "Clovis" in France)? Or is it secular (as in the powerful rise of the "Enlightenment" and the promotion of rationalism)? Having failed to define a European identity, we never drafted a "preamble." We allowed our convictions to dissolve, our intents to disunite, our energies to be sapped. We did not vote to approve the European Constitution: we undid Europe. And Europe has never recovered. Yet what *makes* Europe Europe is, of course, that it is both Christian *and* secular (and other things as well). It is that Europe developed *in the divide* between the two: in the great divide between reason and religion, faith and the Enlightenment. In the *interspace* between the two – an "interspace" that has nothing to do with compromise, nothing to do with a simple between-the-two, and everything to do with tension between the two, tension that quickens the one and the other. Hence the requirement of faith has been honed by divide on the requirement of reason, and vice versa (indeed, within a single mind: Pascal's). Hence the richness or resource that "makes Europe Europe" [*fait l'Europe*] – or, better yet, that "yields Europe" [«*fait Europe*»]. In light of the foregoing any definition of European culture, any approach to Europe that centers on identity, is not only terribly reductive and lazy but, indeed, withering, disappointing, and demobilizing.

V

We will defend a culture's resources

I will defend no cultural identity, be it French or European, as if we could define it through difference and set it within an essence. Or as if we could deal with culture in terms of belonging – as if I possessed "my" culture. What I will defend are cultural fecundities, French or European, such as they have deployed in France, or Europe, through inventive divides. I will defend them because I owe them my education and am therefore responsible for both their deployment and their transmission. But they do not therefore become mine to possess. After all, is it not clear that the most attentive stewards of these resources, or fecundities, are often foreigners? Aren't foreigners often more concerned with the French language's resources and proper usage than many so-called "native" French? Yet it is true, as Nietzsche remarked, that a culture always sees the light of day and develops in a certain atmosphere, in a certain milieu. It always advenes locally, within a vicinity, and in a land-scape: in a language and an ambiance, the latter serving to imbue [*formant prégnance*]. Through the singular, then, for only the singular is crea-tive. Culture's deployment is circumstantial: the Florence of the Medici, or the Jewish Vienna of the late nineteenth century, but also the third- and fourth-century lettered court of the Wei and the Jin, the eighth- to tenth-century Baghdad of the Abbasids, and enlightened twelfth-century Andalusia, when and where "philosophy" was a word uttered in Arabic: *falsafa*. But these resources are thereafter available to all. We will return to this.

I defend these resources all the more now that they are under threat. In this resistance there are two fronts, which I have already sketched. The first lies where the uniform now serves as semblance and simulacrum of the universal, the second where the common has lost the under-pinning of the universal and has flipped into its opposite (the self-segregation of communities, or "*communautarisme*"). To one side we must resist the impoverishment of cultures, the cultural flattening occasioned by global and commercial uniformization. Here it is the market that "yields a world" [«*fait monde*»]. The same Harry Potter books lie stacked everywhere on the planet at the same instant, casting children's imaginations in an identical mold – and, to boot, increasingly doing it in the same Globish. The first stand to make must be for the *multiplicity* of languages. If we begin to speak only one tongue, if the fertile divides between languages are lost, then languages will no longer be able to reflect off one another: they will no longer enable the perception of one another's *resources*. Soon we will be unable to think outside of the same standardized notions, and begin to mistake mere stereotypes of thought for universals. "Babel" is, in fact, a stroke of good fortune for thought. Without it we would bring about our own dispossession. By silent transformation, in exchange for greater ease in communication, we would trade away the resources of thought – resources that are in the first place *lingual*: that lie in the diversity of languages and their inventive divides. We would cease to translate. We would dwell no more in the ever-so-fertile interspace between languages, where the possibilities of one language are put to proof and revealed in another, and vice versa. In that interspace where the translator can open one language by means of another, pull it from its conformity, call forth its capacities. We are sounding the alarm at present over the planet's "biodiversity" and the exhaustion of its natural resources. Why are we not equally concerned by the exhaustion of these other resources?

To the other side we must resist the threat that the common – at any scale: nation, continent, world – will flip into its opposite: the self-segregation of communities [*communautarisme*]. It is evident that beyond a certain threshold, if a given community ceases to integrate, the sharing that gives rise to the common will be undone and turn into its opposite. It will flip into sectarianism and identitarian withdrawal. Or, worse, if it turns offensive, into a will to exclude and destroy. The two sides are linked, of course. Identity claims are an expression of the repression brought about by the world's uniformization, and the attendant false universal. A process that, as we know, is primarily economic and financial. From that point on the failure of integration flips into fundamentalism, a violent case in point being Islamism in France. As a result, the shared cultural common in the country (France), the common that *yields* the country, fractures until it falls apart. Unless we muster a defense there will come a day, perhaps in the not too distant future, when Molière and Pascal will be banished from the schools, lest they offend convictions. More fundamentally, knowing the common language – French, with classical French included – will no longer suffice. But what does it mean to "defend"? To defend resources is above all to activate them, and not just to take up a trepidatious, defensive stance. It is chiefly by developing (activating) knowledge of French as the elementary, common resource of all French people, or the reading of Molière (or Rimbaud) as a resource of shared intelligence, that we will effectively deploy France's cultural common. In particular by doing so from a diversity of resources, rather than clinging to some fantastical identity.

Indeed, we must pause to consider the consubstantial plurality of the concept of "resources." There is no French or European cultural identity. There are only *resources* (French, European, and,

43

of course, other). Identities are defined, resources inventoried. Resources are explored and exploited (*activated*, in my parlance). The requirement of universality is indeed a resource (even if, as we have seen, its line of thought is not universal but singular). It is a resource, as we have seen, through its "regulatory" capacity: its capacity indefinitely to promote the common in History and keep it open, despite the common's inclination to shut itself in and wall itself off. In fact, resources by their nature have a capacity for *promotion*. To approach it from the most general perspective, another European resource, correlative to universality, is, it seems to me, the promotion of the Subject: not of the individual (or of individualism as folded back upon the narrowness of its *I*) but of the subject as a "self" that is uttered and thereby introduces its initiative into the world, carries into the world a purpose that opens a breach in the world's wall: and thus makes it "abide outside [*tenir hors*]" the enclosure of a world and properly "ex-ist." This translates politically into the resource, forever in need of liberation, that is the subject's liberty. Democracy – though still struggling to find its constitution – draws from this its rationale and legitimacy. For democracy is primarily a matter of treating others as subjects: that is, of promoting a community of subjects. Thus its genius, ever since the Greeks, has been its capacity to convince the other with speech (*peithein*). You address the other as you would a subject endowed with initiative and liberty – that is, an equal – rather than seek to get him under your influence or resort to violence. Only persuasion, as Plato knew, can serve as an alternative to brute force.

Suppose we wanted not to define Europe but to sketch out a field of heritages and coherencies that "yield" Europe, a field forever to be excavated and tilled. We could begin by examining all the terms whose semantics are common to the great European language. Born of painting, *paysage* is a European word (think of *paesaggio* and *paisaje*, as well as *Land-schaft* and *land-scape*, not to mention the Russian). It speaks to the promotion of "land" ("*pays*") into "landscape" ("*paysage*"). In this sense landscape is also a *resource*. China, the other great landscape culture, opens a divide with respect to these semantics by saying "mountain(s)-water(s)" (*shan-shui*), the correlation of the High and the Low (or of the immobile and the mobile, of form and formlessness, etc.). China, then, offers another resource – one just as coherent and just as power-ful, but one that we did not conceive of, or even imagine, from within Europe. It offers another angle from which to enter into the thought of what we call "landscape." "Ideal" is another word found in all European languages (even, I believe, in Hungarian, which is not Indo-European). It speaks to an essential resource: our ability to produce an ideal (abstract) representation and promote it into an "ideal" by making it into the object of our aspiration (for Plato desire, *erôs*, con-nects to the form-model, *eidos*). The resource of the ideal has occasioned Europe's deployment by erecting itself into a vocation, and has even led to the idea of revolution, in art as in politics. Has the resource of the ideal now run dry? We observe, in any case, that a language–line of thought such as Chinese has not set forth this plane of ideality. The modern-Chinese neologism *li-xiang* (ideal) only borrows from European language and grafts on a new meaning: because, indeed, cultural resources – those of language first – are borrowed and imported and do not belong.

We must therefore rethink the relation between the subject and culture when the culture in ques-tion is not "his" culture; or, rather, when the possessive is one of appropriation (learning)[1] and not of possession (sharing excluded). For it seems to me that cultural identity has received tacit but undue support from an equivocation. We tend to confuse improperly posited cultural identity with the (psychological) principle of identification. Cultural identity would seem to have thrived on this amalgam.

Identification derives its legitimacy from the subject's formative process (a child might grow up identifying, often ambivalently, with his father), but culture does not. For one thing, culture, as a collective creation, is forever becoming more diverse and heterogeneous; it will not be reduced to some singular figure (such as the "Father"), or even to some unitary feature that could serve as an object of assimilation and investment. For another, the subject's relation to culture is one of learning and acquisition, not self-justification; culture is not to help the subject construct an image of his self in his quest for acknowledgment – or else it would be a perverted use of culture (as in the rise of Nazism). As a set of resources, culture seeks, on the contrary, to promote a subject's *existential* capacity, which is above all his capacity for *dis-adherence*, that source of consciousness. It seeks to promote the subject precisely by compelling it to overflow the wall of his self and withdraw from his integration in a world; and thus to hoist himself "out of" (*ex*) any vassal-like relation to them and clear out some liberty – what I call proper "ex-istence."

In consequence, the subject is responsible for the cultural resources that enable him to promote himself into a subject in the first place. Cultural resources, like any other kind, can be set aside. We can lose them, neglect them, stop maintaining them. They revert to weedy wasteland. Consider the "elegance" still deployed in France not so very long ago. Is it lost forever? To judge by today's television shows,[2] we have let it languish. We can allow the resources of language as well to fall into escheat. As I have said, resources exist only insofar as we activate them. To avoid using the subjunctive is to lose the resource by which we detach the ideal from the factual, the better to discern the mode through which a subject chooses to relate to the real (to what "real"?). Or consider the philosophy essay on France's Baccalaureate examination, teaching students to weigh pros and cons and construct an inquiry. This is a primary resource for effective, egalitarian access to citizenship. Every time it comes under threat we must recall the need for it: not in the name of some "cultural exception" but because it works. Or consider the teaching of Latin and Greek, to which the Ministry of Education has just dealt a death blow in France.[3] The former association of these languages with bourgeois ideology and class elitism (the traditional *lycée* education) in no way obviates their formative value: to hone subjects' skill in language overall and cause their intellectual horizons to overflow (as pedagogical trials in difficult suburbs[4] have shown). We have abandoned Latin and Greek in France out of false modernism and false democratism: that is, demagoguery and historical cowardice. We will have to teach them again.

One might believe these to be minor matters. The subjunctive, the philosophy class, Latin: how can they compare with the present danger, the fundamentalist menace we are now faced with? But there are in fact no "small" resources. Resources by their nature rise to the surface in a local and unforced way, but this is also why they are directly at hand, serving right at the level of experience. Resources are not brandished. They are not slogans to be chanted, and differ in this respect from "values." But *values*, global as they are, demand an adhesion tributary to some unknown that we will always wonder about. Is this adhesion perhaps a bit arbitrary, or in any case relative? Might it stem from some deeper, more secret adherence, so murky at bottom that we will struggle to justify it? For this reason values run the risk of tipping back into the cultural identification I have just denounced. Resources, meanwhile, are not ideological (are not built up into "systems"). They are reckoned by their effects alone, by the gains to be had from them. Their validity – for lack of pompous truth – is self-evident. (It's their validity that is *index sui*.) Resources are not "advocated"; we needn't preach them – unlike values, which call for conversion, or at least approval. Moreover, values contradict one another and are even exclusive. If I adhere to "Christian values" I will have a hard time adhering to atheist values, or else I will have to compromise. Resources, however, are not exclusive. I can gain indifferently from these or those. They are additive and non-limiting. I have spent decades exploiting the resources of Chinese thought, and there is no end to it. They do not belong, as I have said, but are available to all. They go to whoever takes the trouble to exploit them.

I will therefore speak of Christian *resources* rather than of the Christian "roots" we hear so much about. The image of the root is suspect, as are all treatments of culture in terms of the natural world. The "root" steers us away from historical representation. It then leads us to forget how Christianity partook in History once it served as the dominant ideology – once it was established as a state religion: "*la France toute catholique*,"[5] dogmatically and politically unified, tolerating no further divide ("one king, one law, one faith"). And what do non-Christians have to do with "Christian roots" – or with "Christian values," for that matter? But that there are resources to explore and exploit in Christianity seems to me an elementary observation. In fact, it's high time we approached Christianity from outside the believer/non-believer schism, leaving aside the question of God and his "existence" (has it not by now run its course?); from outside the alternatives of faith and atheism; and instead consider what Christianity has *promoted* within the human. This is, however, no facile reduction to its mere "anthropological" content (in the manner of a Feuerbach). We are to view Christianity as a resource partaking in the *existential promotion of the subject*. Not just how it dared to explore the exceeding [*dépassement*] of the Law (through "love"), or the reversal of reason (the "madness" of the Cross), thereby erecting a paradoxical logic that set existence into tension. But also how it deployed the "conscience" as the subject's intimate tribunal, opening the subject's subjectivity to the infinite, or how it led us to reconsider our relation to life; we were no longer to seek the "good" life – the qualified, "ethical" life of the Greeks – but life as "life," as living life (qualified in this sense as "eternal"). In this Christianity opens a *divide* with Judaism, brings to light a new possibility. But Judaism has not therefore reached its expiry or historical end. Christianity maintains itself through its *tension* with Judaism.

VI

From divides to the common

Unlike the "narcissism of small differences" that jealously withdraws into fantastical identities, cultural *divides* are deployments that open the way to new possibilities and reveal other resources. They pull culture from the rut of its tradition, pull thought from its comforting dogmatism (its right-mindedness), and set the mind forth once more into adventure. The steamroller of global uniformization, driven by the law of the market, tends to flatten and blur cultural differences, reducing them to an eternal fac-simile. If we are to resist this we must forthwith open new divides: divides into which art and politics, as well as philosophy, must venture. But not in a fictive or projected, declaredly utopian way.

A divide – insofar as it opens, where and for as long as it opens – is effective from the start. To philosophize, as Parmenides already posited, is to make a departure [*s'écarter*].[1] It is to veer from the beaten paths of opinion, step back from the accepted and the agreed-upon, clear a new way – bore – into thought, and do it afresh. We take no interest in how Aristotle's thought differs from Plato's, as the inquiry would lead us to set each into the fixity of a system and place it in a niche (Platonism or Aristotelianism). The important thing – the significant thing – is how Aristotle opens a divide with respect to Plato, how he attempts, in dissidence, to break through what stands in resistance to thought. In other words, open a new path to the unthought-of. In this way Aristotle's thought sets Plato's into tension, rather than let it turn facile and sink into the cliché of Platonism. Aristotle's thought, from its remove, makes Platonism emerge anew, puts it into starker relief. There opens between them an interspace for dialogue. The more divides open post-Plato with respect to Plato, the greater Plato's thought becomes as a resource, the more it is activated. What, after all, is a philosophical library if not the juxtaposition of so many divides

setting thought into tension and thereby indefinitely unfolding and deploying the thinkable?

The concept of the *divide* enables us to think
out the origin as it is – an evolving, unfixed
thing – and stop conferring on it the status of
myth. Rather than have us posit a common
genre – stable, definitive in constitution, as if
coming out of nowhere and impossible to account
for ("man," "human nature," or "common
ground"); a unitary genre, with an identity, and
from which the diversity of cultures would subse-
quently unfold (the sort of genre that difference
posits) – the divide sets us down right away in a
transformation, within a genesis and an advent.
It is a historical (emergence-tracing), rather
than metaphysical (essence-fixing), concept.
Difference is resultative and therefore static. The
divide, meanwhile, is, in its soaring,[2] dynamic.
In other words, rather than have us first posit
a "human nature" without our knowing where
it came from or what it is, the divide elucidates
the promotion of what *becomes man* – and in
so doing already establishes a remove by succes-
sive divides with respect to earlier "Homininae"
("Australopithecus," "Paranthropus," etc.).
"Man" *appeared by divide* and by divide began

55

to "ex-ist." It is by "ex-aptation" – that is, by egress from the preceding adaptation – that an unhooking [*décrochage*] processually took place and carried what would become man toward his development. It is, incidentally, here and there, in separated [*écartés*] places, that paleontologists observe man's apparition. I no longer set out as my point of departure the term "human nature" – that unitary-identitarian term, so ideological in definition – but neither need I establish a primordial separation between "nature" and "culture" – terms so abstractly (arbitrarily) dissociated. I consider the diversity of cultures to be a self-deployment of the human that prolongs the divide that specifically occasioned its advent and that each particular divide, opened *existentially* by a subject, still permits us to activate and deploy.

To understand this self-deployment of the human we must yet understand what *écart*[3] means. The common English translation of *écart* is *gap*. But *écart* means the opposite of *gap*. *Gap* denotes a pit that separates, whereas *écart* denotes a distance that opens and establishes a face-off [*met en regard*], brings forth an *interspace* [*de l'« entre »*] that sets into tension what has been separated and compels each side to gaze keenly at the other [*se dévisager*]. Because this divergence was underappreciated, there was for a few years a general and rather amusing misapprehension of my work. It was understood in reverse. In my philosophical drydock[4] I have sought to fathom the full extent of the divides of both language and thought between the cultures of China and Europe, considering them as so many resources for thought. I have sought to prevent sham "equivalencies" from obscuring the fortunate diversity of our language and thought, sought to draw each line of thought out of its atavism, perturb its habitus, and give thought something to think about again. But I have not, of course, sought to isolate these cultures from each other, shut them inside their bubbles, and "essentialize" them. (What I call "Chinese thought" – need I remind the reader? – is simply thought expressed in Chinese. As a philosopher I allow myself to detach the coherencies of Chinese thought from their context, abstract them, and develop them into concepts.) Nor have I sought to "compare" them, in terms of resemblance or difference, as seems possible when we restrict ourselves to arraying and identifying. Rather, I have sought to establish various vis-à-vis (across the divides I have located) and set the languages and cultures to reflect each other: so as to undertake a *deconstruction* from without and get an oblique handle on our unthought-of.

Meanwhile, it is difference, hand in hand with identity, that isolates and "essentializes" cultures. It is difference that drives us into the impasse of universalism or of relativism. And there is no escaping the alternative thereafter. On the one hand, we can rank cultural difference after identity (the identity of human nature, or our "common ground"). But this unity-identity raised to a principle is one that I project from my own cultural perspective. It is, in other words, nothing but a product of my ethnocentrism. I have retained the cultural categories that I deem beforehand to be universal. This is the *facile universalism* that I denounced at the start. On the other hand (otherwise), we can rank cultural difference first, with each culture folding back into its supposed identity. Here we cannot help but shut these cultures into worlds. This is "culturalism," which prepares the way for a *lazy relativism* that never seeks to exceed its own bounds [*se dépasser*]. It is but the reverse of the false universal – false because too quickly accorded and not developed over the course of an inquiry that, as I have said, is never satisfied but effectively induces the common to deploy.

Difference lets each of the terms fall to its wayside, into its isolation, but the divide sets the terms face to face, holds in tension what it has separated, and, therefore, alone can effectively produce the *common*: an active and intensive common. Each term, entering into a relation with the other, sheds its self-sufficiency in the *interspace* opened by divide, spills over the wall of its in-itself-ness [*son quant-à-soi*]. Recall, however, that *the common is not the similar* and that we must translate it to a political plane: integration is not assimilation. The integration of newcomers that every society rightly demands – if it hopes to avoid disassociation, especially after waves of immigration – signifies integration into a shared common: the common of language as well as of history, of cultural touchstones as well as modes of intelligence transmitted by education, of arts and ways of life. The *common*, that is, of *resources*. But this common is not one of assimilation by reduction to the similar. After all, what exactly is the typical "Frenchman," normalized in his morality, clothes, and behavior, that we see so often invoked? If culture has no identitarian essence, what can he be but a statistical average or a reproduction of clichés that endure only as stereotypes? The *common* cannot be a matter of cloning or repetition, cannot be a banality, if it is to retain its *fecundity*.

What, in effect, keeps a society together? What promotes and deploys it (as when we say "French society")? What confers its soaring and consistency? Its *con-sistency* is not made of differences *or* resemblances, or of resemblances more than of differences: resemblances that color differences or differences that resorb into resemblances. Nor is it made of "multiple identity": that latest way to recover and modulate identity by attuning it to a diversity that is no longer unifiable. It is not a matter of adjusting the needle between these opposites; of setting it more aptly between *less* or *more* of the required assimilation; of choosing between a more open and tolerant and a more closed and intransigent integration. A society's consistency is attributable *both* to its capacity for divides and to its shared common: a shared common deployed and set to work by the divides that make it active and productive, keep it from bogging down in a norm, prevent its atrophy – impel it towards renewal. The relation between the two is thus not one of distribution, dosage, and proportion. It is one of tension, the sole possible factor of intensity and promotion. Neither of the two has ontological priority, but one is the other's condition. It is in the common that divides deploy; at the same time, it is divides that deploy the common.

The current risk that French society will dis-integrate, as the increasing self-segregation of communities [*communautarisme*] undoes the common, serves as a brutal reminder of the need to think through the conditions of our "living together" [« *un vivre ensemble* »]. The expression seems inevitable, the old Greek term (*sy-zēn*) having suddenly gained new currency. The Greeks were already teaching that the Polis is no mere community of place, is not established merely to protect individuals and favor trade, but is founded on the "deliberate choice" of living together. Such is its purpose (*telos*). But what does this choice consist of? Tolerance and compromise, as the preaching goes? Each attenuating his values and convictions, the singularity of his experiences, so as to smooth out divergences and cohabitate without too much friction? Or might a society not instead deploy *through* [au travers] the divides between the things it can keep *face to face* [en regard], one side turned actively toward the other, and both cooperating in the common – without seeking to "exceed" [*« dépasser »*] or resorb the divides? Divides between ages and perspectives (within the family, to start with), functions and occupations, regions and environments. Paris is beautiful in its divides between landscapes and arrondissements. The language of the suburbs or of youth, when not a mere shrinking of resources through negligence or ignorance, awakens (heightens) the language from its academism through the invention of using (daring to use)[5] divides. If it still has any meaning, if it is not merely a veil drawn over the unsightliness to avoid a clash,[6] we must think of "dialogue" in terms of the tension that generates the common from the divide and the face-off. Divides that do not close up into differences of identity but open the *interspace* for a new common arise.

VII

Dia-logue

We have imagined every which way the famous "dialogue of cultures." We have dreamed in particular of a *synthesis*, the world's cultures coming into accord and completing one another in a unified set. This is the dream of a happy concord in which divergences are erased and the common overwhelms the diverse by absorbing it. We have complacently projected this image between "East" and "West," erecting them as the poles of human experience, the great symbolic marriage. Two cultures supposed to have risen on opposite slopes and meeting at the summit. But in what language – by means of what notional and syntactical tool – will this coupling take place? Within the Western categories that have now been globalized and reduced to Globish? The diverse cultures of the world will now be mere exotic variants. Though the new globalized culture presents itself as the world's parliament, promising to be representative and democratically to embrace the various currents, we still will not have questioned the cultural framework, implicit and illusively universal because proceeding from a veiled uniformization, in which the assembly takes place. And, like all syntheses, it will have resorbed the tensions, blurred the divides, and become terribly boring. And the resulting common, moreover, will be artificial: it will not have set the diverse to work, that it might *promote itself* into the common.

Or else it will seek to elucidate an authentic common – authentic because primordial – by looking for a *common denominator* between cultures. The inverse of synthesis being analysis, we will decompose the full diversity of cultures into basic elements and look for overlaps. Should we find no hard, identical core, we will seek to discern at least a common in the form of a "comparable relation" between terms, a sort of interaction or mediation by "analogy." To help fashion a global, now planetary ethic, UNESCO worked diligently in the final decades of the twentieth century to identify points of concord. One such minimal element, supposedly beyond doubt, is the notion that all moral conceptions and all religious traditions, worldwide, advocate "peace": "a vision of peoples living peacefully together."[1] Who, after all, wouldn't want peace? – But what about Hegel? What about Heraclitus? Did they not explicitly call for war to bring out the function – indeed, the ethical function – of the negative? Not only does any reduction of the diversity of cultures to some minimal, supposedly common element drag us down to the banality of truisms, but, worse, the "truisms" aren't even true.[2] A more significant logic escapes them. Whereas the complementarity of cultures might always turn out to be the product of preliminary if unsuspected assimilation, overlaps between cultures might always turn out to be superficial, because they miss what is most singular in each culture. Whether through complementarity or overlaps, the arbitrary resorption of divides strips cultures of their inventive resources.

We have also more seriously – more philosophically – tried something else: to dig down to some ultimate grounding of reason, below all the traditional paradigms of truth (adequation with things, or self-evidence to our awareness), to find a *logical* common for humanity. The community of men as "communicational" community is to be sought, more radically, in the very conditions of possibility for sensible discourse (the path set forth by Apel and Habermas). The rules of usage in language are rules we implicitly recognize as valid as soon as we speak. They are thus, *a priori*, rules that men share. Because we put these rules to pragmatic use as soon as we speak, whether to ourselves or to others, the consensus among men proceeds not from any content but purely from the form of our statements [*l'énoncé*][3] and from what they necessarily take to be their requisites, which as such are universals. This no doubt holds as long as we remain within the framework of the European *logos* as the Greeks conceived of its requirements (Aristotle's principle of non-contradiction, to begin with). But if we step outside Europe? Doesn't the discursive cunning of a Chinese thinker like Zhuangzi lie precisely in the ability to foil the supposedly common logic of communication (thus we'd have to "find someone who has forgotten speech to speak with")? Or consider the Zen paradox (the *kōan*). Is it not the Zen strategy to cause a sudden breach and thereby implode the implicit protocols of rationality? Can we afterwards still engage in "dialogue"? If we call dialogue's very protocol into question do we not irredeemably abandon the very principle of concord between men, the foundational cultural common?

"Dialogue," in truth, has itself been stained with suspicion historically. First of all, the West has engaged in "dialogue" with other cultures because of its lost power. Back in the day, riding high not just on its "universal" values but especially on its logical formalization, the West would not engage in dialogue. It would impose its universalism on other cultures: that is, it would colonize them with its triumphant rationality. Indeed, isn't "dialogue" a lenitive term concealing the endless power struggles that take place between cultures as well as within individual languages and cultures, with the prevailing coherencies overshadowing and burying the others? Does dialogue pretend to a false irenism, or cloak itself in a false egalitarianism? Moreover – the question arises once again – in what language is dialogue to take place? If in a single language (say, globalized English, or Globish), then the dialogue is skewed from the start. When cultures meet on the terrain of a single language – within its syntactical forms and categories – other languages and cultures can air their "differences" only *secondarily*, from the generic common that is supposed to expedite communication. There often follow exceedingly virulent identity claims, because by then there remains no other riposte to a uniformization imposed in advance.

Yet without dialogue we get "shocks" and clashes. Is there a way out of the dilemma? Or, if it seems a stopgap to avoid open violence, how can we give dialogue a consistency to dignify it and establish it as a vocation? If it is a "soft" term, we must give it a strong sense; and, once again, the best way to go about this is to draw directly from language and sound its resource. In Greek *dia* means both divide and crossing. A *dia*-logue is all the more fecund, as the Greeks already knew, for having a divide in play (as in the potent dialogue between Socrates and Callicles). If we say more or less the same thing, the dialogue turns into a monologue for two, and the mind makes no progress. But *dia* has another meaning: path that crosses a space, with the space perhaps offering up resistance. A dia-logue is not instantaneous;

it takes time. Only gradually, patiently, can the respective positions – separate and distant as they are – discover each other, reflect each other, and slowly develop the conditions of possibility for an effective encounter. Things must unfold. Meanwhile, *logos* speaks to the common of the intelligible, which serves paradoxically as both the condition and the aim of dia-logue. In other words, a common is engendered through the divides themselves. Each language, each line of thought, each position allowing itself to spill over because of the other, a mutual intelligence can emerge in an *interspace* that has become active – even if said intelligence is never fully realized (the potential in the *intelligible* speaks to this). This common is no matter of resorption of divides or forced assimilation. Rather, it is *produced*, as the internal tension of the divides occasion work. Neither imposed nor held to be given from the start, it is *promoted*.

By calling forth each perspective bit by bit, and reciprocally, from its exclusivity – not from its position, mind you, but from its obstructed, walled-in character; from its ignorance of the other – dia-logue brings about the gradual emergence of a shared field of intelligence, where each can begin to hear the other. But where does the effect of intelligence come from, and what makes it constraining (what takes us past the complacency of wishful thinking)? The answer is that each perspective undoes not its position but its position's exclusionary nature, and starts to set the other's position face to face with its own.

By integrating the other's position within its own horizon, each in effect sets its own perspective into tension, withdrawing that perspective from its *solitary self-evidence*. By abandoning the purely defensive view of the other's position and viewing it instead from the angle of emergent possibilities – by listening to the other, from the exterior that *is* the other – each comes to perceive its own position, and consequently discovers that it is unilateral. The position of each is unsealed, and by discreet shift a displacement begins. Once dialogue is engaged (if, of course, it is not an act or counterfeit) and for as long as it lasts (Plato's Callicles prefers to withdraw, his Philebus never to enter) an *interspace* comes to light – each position opening slightly to the other (as in the *enter* of *enter-tain*)[4] – in which thought once more gets down to work. Through this *interspace* thought passes once more and can

be activated. Far from complacent, or merely lenitive in effect, dia-logue alone is operative *in itself*
as an instrument. Without it one always forces
the other to assimilate – in other words, brings
about its "alienation" – and the power struggle
will continue.

But in what language, at the world's scale, is
the dialogue between cultures to take place? If it
cannot occur in the language of either perspective without provoking the other's alienation, the
answer is, for once, simple: dialogue can occur
only in the languages of both the one and the
other: in other words, between the two languages, in the *interspace* opened by translation.
Because there is no third-party or mediating language (globalized English, or Globish, certainly
does not fit the bill), *translation* is the *logical*
language for dialogue. Or, to borrow a well-
known phrase (though I am transferring it from
Europe to the world), translation ought to be
the world's language. The world to come ought
to be the inter-lingual world: not the world of
a dominant language, whatever it might be, but
that of translation as it activates the resources of
various languages with respect to one another.
Languages both discovering one another and get-

ting back down to work, that something might pass between them. A single language would be much more convenient, certainly, but it would also impose its uniformization. Exchange would be made easier, but there would be nothing, or nothing effectively singular, left to exchange. Once all is arrayed in a language, with no further divides to disturb it, every language / line of thought – every culture – will, as I have said, be reduced to stubborn declarations of its identitarian "differences." Translation, however, is dia-logue carried out in a basic and convincing way. It allows for dia-logue's discomfort, indefinite character, repeated attempts, and chronic incompleteness, but also for dia-logue's measure of the effective. A common of intelligence develops and deploys in translation's *interspace*.

Intelligence as developed by the diversity of language and thought is not a finite, arrested understanding (like the Kantian understanding of categories). The more it is called upon to venture across diverse intelligibilities, as in the dia-logue of cultures, the more it is called upon to promote itself: the more intelligent it becomes. One of the benefits of our era, counter to worldwide uniformization, is that we can discover other languages and other cultures, opening ourselves up to other coherencies and thus to other modes of intelligibility. Particularly for Europe: in its encounters with other languages and other cultures European thought needn't reverse its former sufficiency – that of its universalism – into a guilty conscience, or even into mere relativism. Nor need it undergo a conversion (into some artificial "Far East"). But it has the opportunity to inquire into itself from the outside, and thereby return its reason to drydock.[5] For it is in the name of a logical universal, a universal in the strong sense, *a priori*, and not by invoking some (necessarily ideo-logical) definition of man or human nature, that I set forth a common of the intelligible. This *common of the intelligible* is the *common of the human*. Though men or cultures never understand one another completely, we must nevertheless set it forth as a principle – as an *a priori* necessity (as a *transcendental* necessity of the human) – that they *can* understand one another; and it is this possibility alone of understanding the diversity of the human – as through languages – that yields the "human."

Furthermore, I do not see the subject-to-come as some as yet unknown – as yet unborn – figure of the subject: awaiting another Revelation or a new Truth. In our now-completed world (the further we explore it, the more complete it is) where would this hope for an Elsewhere come from? I see this subject-to-come as one that is no longer a *vassal* [*qui n'est plus* inféodé]: no longer prisoner to a particular truth, to a truth-in-a-"nutshell,"[6] delivered through dogma and, as such, exclusive. Nor do I see the subject-to-come, inversely, as *de-territorialized*, and cut off from the local and the singular – from a language, culture, and landscape. I see the subject-to-come as *agile* – or, let us say, "alert" (the opposite of "inert": i.e., artless and thus lethargic). I see him as coming from one language and a certain milieu and circulating among other languages and other milieus, and drawing on their respective resources; as neither mixing (confusing) the diversity of cultures and forms of intelligence nor reducing them – this amounts to the same thing – to a more consensual and declaredly "tolerant" version. A cultural form is significant through the divides and singularities, and thus the invention, it produces. It will have drawn lines of thought in their diversity out of their initial exclusiveness and had them contribute to a common of intelligence. "Dia-logue" consists precisely of this.

These days, in a world all but globalized, with no Beyond to dream of or a Far-Off to travel to anymore, it is indeed in the *interspace* that the resource is to be found. The term "inter-cultural," if it have any meaning at all, must mean to deploy *interspace* and enter-tainment [*entre-tien*][7] as the new dimension of the world and of culture. Thus the false (lazy) universality of the uniform and the correlative (sectarian) fantasy of identity are undone. If to ex-ist is to resist – that is, first of all to "abide outside of" [« *se tenir hors* »], outside what is undergone, especially what is undergone in History – and if every era has its own resistance, then let us posit that our era's struggle is to cede not an inch of ground to the twin perils of uniformization and identity, and to inaugurate, through the inventive power of the divide, an intensive common.

Translator's Notes

Preface
1 This book was written prior to the 2017 French presidential election – *Ed.*
2 A sociological phenomenon known in France as *communautarisme*. [All notes by the translator unless otherwise specified.]
3 I.e., progress in the sense of heading down a path.

I The universal, the uniform, the common
1 English speakers call this general history.
2 A world's fair.
3 See note 2, in the preface.

II Is the universal an outmoded notion?
1 A reference to Michel Foucault's book *L'Archéologie*

du savoir, translated into English as *The Archaeology of Knowledge*.

2 The French reads: "*avec ce que ce « sur » (« à propos de ») laisse entendre de distance par son surplomb.*" *Porter sur* means "carry on to" in the literal sense and "deal with" in common usage. The *on* (*sur*), the author writes, conveys something like "distance from above" ("*distance par son surplomb*").

3 Galatians 3:28, King James translation.

4 The French adjective/participle *tendu* can mean outstretched/proffered (as in "*tendre la main*": "reach for a handshake") or tense (in the sense of tension). Here it introduces the first meaning while also harking back to the tension-setting [*mise en tension*] of the divide [*écart*].

5 This is the author's notion of work [*travail*]. Anything that remains amenable to change will "work" to that end, and is thus alive. The changeless – the self-satisfied, the walled-in, the isolated, anything not exposed to a divide – is dead.

III Difference or divide: identity or fecundity

1 *Écart* has multiple meanings not all of which are covered by the English word *divide*. Here, then, the translation draws from another of the author's special terms, *detour* [*détour*], which is closely related to his notion of the *écart*. In the author's sense a detour is the journey one takes across a divide to a second culture, from there to look back upon one's own.

2 The French reads: "*que « quelque chose » effectivement passe (se passe)*." That is, French provides a parallel between *pass* (*passer*) and *happen* (*se passer*).

IV There is no such thing as cultural identity

1 *Underground* and *off* appear in English in the original text.

V We will defend a culture's resources

1 Especially in the United States, the term *cultural appropriation* has come to mean something like cultural theft. This is not what the author means. (Note the subsequent parenthesis: *learning*.) Indeed, in many ways the notion of appropriation as theft runs counter to the author's philosophy, in which cultural resources belong to no one.

2 In the original text the word *shows* appears in English, as if to suggest the decadence of French culture through the rise of Frenglish.

3 The administration of President Emmanuel Macron appears as of this writing (in the autumn of 2017) to have reversed the decision.

4 Many of France's most troubled neighborhoods are found not in "inner cities" but in suburbs.

5 A rallying cry whose literal meaning is "wholly Catholic France."

VI From divides to the common

1 The French language allows for a parallel here between

"the divide" (*l'écart*) and "separate oneself" or "make a departure from" (*s'écarter*).

2 *Soaring* [*l'essor*] is a special term in the author's lexicon and stands in opposition to *slackness* [*l'étale*]. What soars is alive, or activated; what is slack, because complete and finished, is dead.

3 Translated throughout, except where noted, as *divide*.

4 The author uses the special term *chantier*, which literally means construction site, or site of industry. In his conception a philosophy is *en chantier* (in workshop conditions) for as long as a philosopher continues to philosophize: that is, for as long as the philosophy continues to evolve, because still alive. (Recall his remark, in chapter IV, about dead languages.) His notion of the *chantier* feeds into his notion of *living* (*le vivre*).

5 Here again the French language allows for a parallel: "*usant (osant)*."

6 *Clash* appears in English in the original text.

VII Dia-logue

1 The phrase appears in English in the original text.

2 The word *true*, elucidating the etymology of *truisms* (*truismes*), appears in English in the original text.

3 I have taken *énoncé*, literally *utterance*, in the broad sense laid out in Foucault's *L'Archéologie du savoir*. Any use of words, spoken or written, would qualify – as, indeed, would any other attempt at communication.

4 Enter-tain (*entre-tenir*) in an etymological sense. The

French reads: "*chaque position s'entre-ouvre à l'autre (tel est l'*entre *de l'« entre-tien »).*" Thus we have parallels between *entre-ouvre*, *l'entre*, and *entre-tien*. The first is commonly used adjectivally as *entrouvert* (also spelled *entr'ouvert*), meaning ajar. *L'entre* is a special term translated throughout as *interspace*. *Entretien* means conversation, discourse, talk, chat. Etymologically (*entre* + *tenir*) it breaks down to inter (between) + hold/sustain. This ties in with the author's notion of the divide (*écart*) as something that, unlike difference, sustains tension indefinitely.

5 The author returns here to his notion of the *chantier*, which I am calling a philosophical drydock: "*remettre sa raison en chantier.*"

6 The author's term in French is *vérité-« bocal »*: literally *"jar"-truth*, *"jarred"-truth*, or perhaps *truth-preserve*.

7 The author returns to the etymological sense of *entre-tien*.